Notre Dame

Cathedral

OUR LADY OF PARIS

A TRAVEL PHOTO ART BOOK

LAINE CUNNINGHAM

Notre Dame Cathedral
Our Lady of Paris
A Travel Photo Art Book

Published by Sun Dogs Creations
Changing the World One Book at a Time
Print ISBN: 9781951389024

Cover Design by Angel Leya
Photo by Ridwan Meah on Unsplash

Copyright © 2019 Laine Cunningham

All rights reserved. No part of this book may be reproduced in any form or by any means, electronic, mechanical, digital, photocopying or recording, except for the inclusion in a review, without permission in writing from the publisher.

THE TRAVEL PHOTO ART SERIES

Ruins of Rome I & II
Along the Via Appia
Garden City Garbatella
Ancients of Assisi I & II
Captivating Capri
Milan Cathedral
Treasures of Turin
Panoramas of Portugal
Linger in Lisbon
The Splendors of Sintra
Spectacles of Stepantsminda
Grandeur in the Republic of Georgia
Tableaus of Tbilisi
Original Old Tbilisi
Marvels of Mtskheta
Paragons of Prague
Hidden Prague
The Pillars of the Bohemian Paradise
Lidice Lives
Terezín and Theresienstadt
Flourishes of France
Portraits of Paris
Notre Dame Cathedral
The Beauty of Berlin

Notre-Dame de Paris, the Notre Dame Cathedral, might be the most famous medieval building in the world. After the 2019 fire, the nickname "Our Lady of Paris" took on new meaning. It became clear that the cathedral belongs to the world.

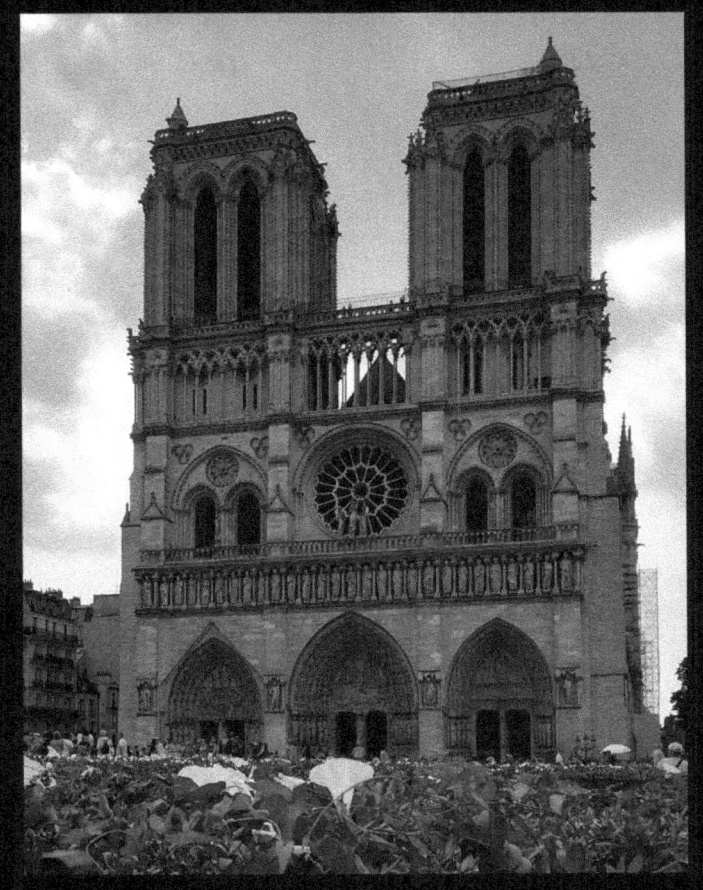

TRUMPET

For centuries, Notre Dame has inspired awe. The flying buttresses rising outside the walls lift all eyes upward. Stone gargoyles transform the mundane task of channeling rainwater with their mythological presence. Hundreds of grotesques peer down, as do numerous statues.

FLIGHT

Adam and Eve are mounted on the west façade along with the Gallery of Kings. The Angel of the Resurrection hovered over the roof. Only days before the fire, sixteen statues were removed from the base of the spire. The twelve apostles and the symbols of the four evangelists were taken down for the first time in 150 years, ensuring their preservation for centuries to come.

APPROACH

Inside, visitors reveled in the cathedral's inspirational proportions. Sunlight streaming through the stained-glass windows splashed the stones with color. The ribbed vaults, left unadorned, divided the upper space. Nothing distracted from the clerestory windows and the arches that made hearts soar.

460 TONS

Astonishingly, the rose windows at the north and south of the cathedral came through the fire. The three windows are masterpieces. The west rose was built in 1125, while the south and north rose windows were created in the thirteenth century. The south rose is the largest, and spans nearly 13 meters, about 42 feet.

EXPLORERS

Unfortunately, other parts of the cathedral met a different fate. The roof and the iconic spire were both lost. The first oak roof frame was built around 1160. Much of that structure was replaced between 1220 and 1240. The vast amount of lumber and beams needed for the project led the roof to be called The Forest.

ALIGHTED

Lead roofing was laid over this framework. The clay normally called upon for roof tiles was too far from Paris to be easily obtained. Instead, thin sheets of lead measuring 5 mm in thickness were crafted. The weight of the lead added 210 tons to the pressure on the walls. The 2019 fire put off yellow smoke due to the lead.

The spire, called la fleche due to its resemblance to an arrow, was added around 1250. Also constructed from wood and lead, it rose over 90 meters, nearly 300 feet. For the next five hundred years, the spire withstood storms and wind. By 1786, it had grown too unstable and was removed.

KING'S BALCONY

In 1844, architect Eugène Emmanuel Viollet-le-Duc was commissioned to restore the cathedral, including the spire. During his career, Viollet-le-Duc gave new life to Mont Saint Michel, Reims Cathedral, Hotel de Cluny, and the City of Avignon. He also designed the internal structure that supports the Statue of Liberty.

When the spire caught fire and collapsed, 750 tons of lead and stone toppled. The bell towers were in peril. The original bells were looted during the French Revolution and melted down into cannonballs. The replacement bells were heavy enough to cause structural damage to the entire cathedral if they fell.

ROSTER

At great personal risk, firemen concentrated their efforts on the north tower. The eight bells housed there could not be allowed to fall. Approaching on the south tower's stairs, they crossed over to the north tower to spray water. Thanks to them, visitors will one day again hear the Emmanuel Bell, one of the most beautiful sound vessels in the world.

The other bells will also ring out. Each bears the name of a saint. They are Marie, Gabriel, Anne Geneviève, Denis, Marcel, Étienne, Benoît-Joseph, Maurice, and Jean-Marie. The smallest weighs more than 1,700 pounds, while the largest weighs nearly 29,260 pounds.

VILLAGE

Many treasures safeguarded by the cathedral were saved. These include the ancient Crown of Thorns relic, which was brought by King Louis IX to Paris. Le Grand Orgue, the organ with 8,000 pipes, is thought to be in working order. The Tunic of Saint Louis, a thirteenth century relic, remains safe.

PILGRIM'S ROUTE

Perhaps the most inspiring items to have survived are the three beehives. Located on top of the sacristy, the wooden boxes stood about a hundred feet below the main roof. The bees would have devoured honey and protected their queen during the fire.

TRANQUIL

Bees are one of the oldest symbols of French royalty. The survival of nearly 200,000 of the noble creatures bodes well for Notre Dame's revival. The Gallic Rooster, or Coq Gaulois, is one of the national emblems of France. Many rejoiced when the rooster that topped the spire was pulled from the rubble intact.

RIDGEBACK

The French government,
private donors and UNESCO,
the cultural agency of the
United Nations, have pledged
to rebuild.

ABOUT THE AUTHOR

Laine Cunningham leads readers around the world. *The Family Made of Dust* is set in the Australian Outback, while *Reparation* is a novel of the American Great Plains. Her travel memoir *Woman Alone* appeals to fans of *Wild* and *Eat Pray Love*.

NOVELS BY
LAINE CUNNINGHAM

The Family Made of Dust

Beloved

Reparation

OTHER BOOKS BY
LAINE CUNNINGHAM

Woman Alone: A Six-Month Journey Through the Australian Outback

On the Wallaby Track

Seven Sisters: Spiritual Messages from Aboriginal Australia

Writing While Female or Black or Gay

Ruins of Rome I & II
Along the Via Appia
Garden City Garbatella
Ancients of Assisi I & II
Captivating Capri
Milan Cathedral
Treasures of Turin
Panoramas of Portugal
Linger in Lisbon
The Splendors of Sintra
Spectacles of Stepantsminda
Grandeur in the Republic of Georgia
Tableaus of Tbilisi
Original Old Tbilisi
Marvels of Mtskheta
Paragons of Prague
Hidden Prague
The Pillars of the Bohemian Paradise
Lidice Lives
Terezín and Theresienstadt
Flourishes of France
Portraits of Paris
Notre Dame Cathedral
The Beauty of Berlin

The Zen of Travel
The Zen of Gardening
Zen in the Stable
The Zen of Chocolate
The Zen of Dogs

The Wisdom of Puppies
The Wisdom of Babies
The Wisdom of Weddings

The Beautiful Book of Questions
The Beautiful Book for Dream Seekers
The Beautiful Book for Rebels
The Beautiful Book for Women
The Beautiful Book for Lovers

www.ingramcontent.com/pod-product-compliance
Lightning Source LLC
Chambersburg PA
CBHW041322110526
44591CB00021B/2873